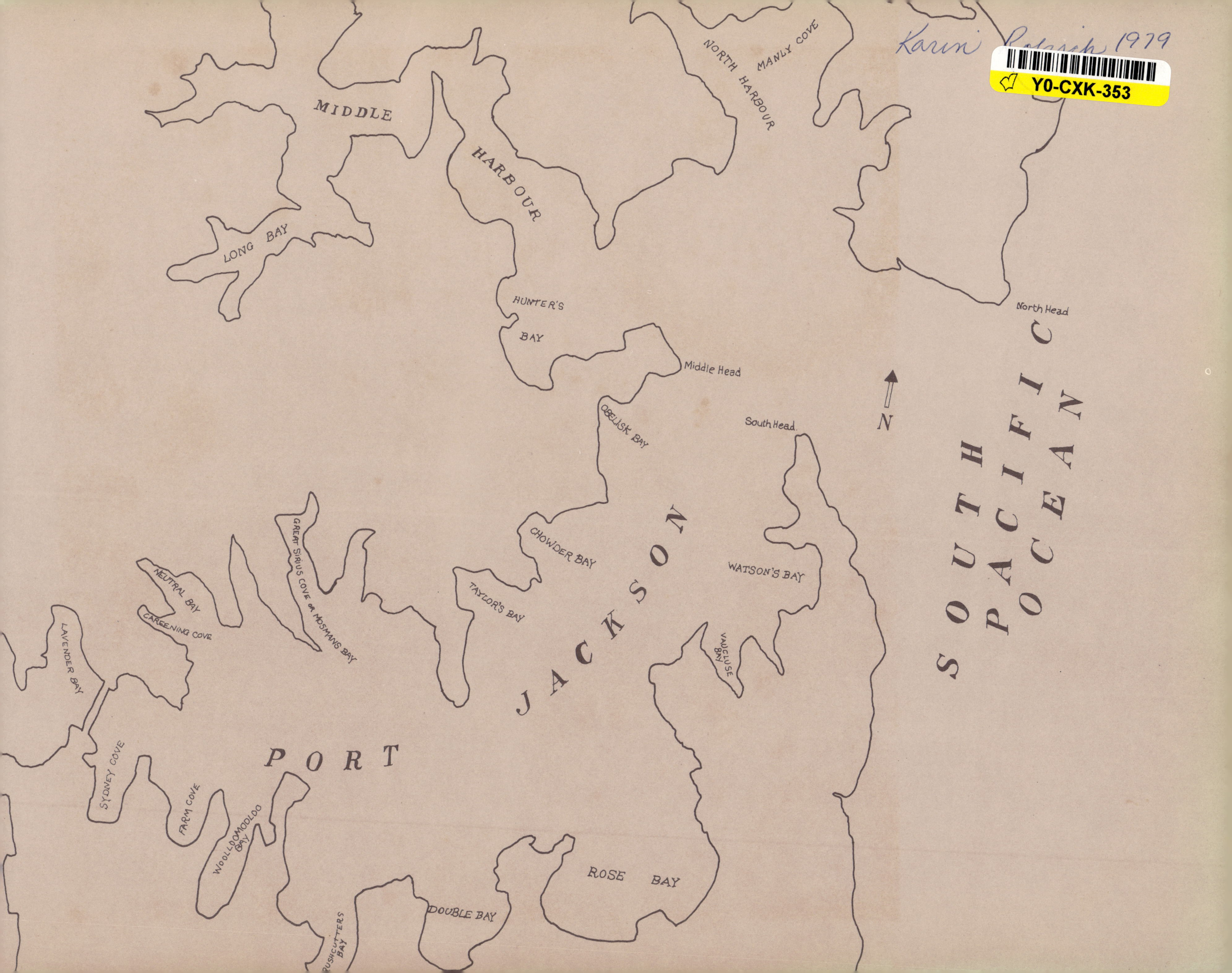
MIDDLE
HARBOUR
LONG BAY
NORTH HARBOUR
MANLY COVE
HUNTER'S BAY
North Head
Middle Head
South Head.
N
OBELISK BAY
SOUTH PACIFIC OCEAN
JACKSON
CHOWDER BAY
WATSON'S BAY
TAYLOR'S BAY
VAUCLUSE BAY
GREAT SIRIUS COVE OR MOSMAN'S BAY
NEUTRAL BAY
CAREENING COVE
LAVENDER BAY
PORT
SYDNEY COVE
FARM COVE
WOOLLOOMOOLOO BAY
ROSE BAY
DOUBLE BAY
RUSHCUTTERS BAY

Sydney Harbour

Paintings from 1794

PORT JACKSON,
New South Wales.
BY
John Septimus Roe, Lieut. R.N.
in 1822.
Note. The Soundings are in Fathoms at Low Water.
HIGH WATER on full and change days about 8h 15' between the Heads / 8.30 in Sydney Cove. Rise of Tide 5 to 8 feet
VARIATION of the Compass observed.
By 16 Azimuths with Theodolite on shore about Sydney Cove 8° 42' E.
By 4 Azimuths d° d° on N.W. end Garden I. 9° 6' E.
By 5 Azimuths d° d° Camp Cove 9° 42' E.
Middle Harbour
North Harbour
Hunters Bay
MIDDLE HEAD
Inner North Head
Outer North Head
Inner South Head
Outer South Head
Camp Cove
Watson's Bay
George's Head
Western Channel
Eastern Channel
Lane Cove
Spectacle I.
Bankes I.
Cockatoo
COCKLE BAY
Iron Stone Cove
Pt. Kiribilli
Garden I.
Clarke I.
Shark I.
Macquarie Tower
LIGHT
SYDNEY
Woollomoolloo
Henrietta Town

Sydney Harbour

Paintings from 1794

Sandra McGrath
Text

Robert Walker
Photography and Research

Introduction John Olsen

The Jacaranda Press

First published 1979 by
THE JACARANDA PRESS

65 Park Road, Milton, Qld.
151 Victoria Road, Gladesville, NSW
83 Palmerston Crescent, South Melbourne, Vic.
142 Colin Street, West Perth, WA
303 Wright Street, Adelaide, SA
4 Kirk Street, Grey Lynn, Auckland 2, NZ

Produced by
THE DAVID ELL PRESS PTY. LTD.
12 Mark Street, Hunters Hill, NSW

Designed by ROY GARWOOD

Book conceived and researched by Robert Walker

National Library of Australia
Cataloguing-in-Publication data
ISBN 0 7016 1254 1

McGrath, Sandra.
Sydney harbour paintings from 1794.

Index
Bibliography
ISBN 0 7016 1254 1
1. Painting, Australian. 2. Sydney—Harbor.
I. Walker, Robert, photographer. II. Title.

759.9'94

Typeset by Modgraphic Pty. Ltd., Adelaide, SA
Printed in Hong Kong.

Artists

Thomas Whitcombe
Britannia in Sydney Cove 1798
Oil on canvas. 81.4 × 120 cm
Rex Nan Kivell Collection, National Library of Australia

Introduction

This book is not only about Sydney Harbour it also shows the beginning of the visual history of Australia, for it is in Sydney that the fledgeling colony began. The fact that this enchanting waterway has continued to inspire artists from colonial to contemporary times is an assurance of its magic.

The Harbour has withstood the mangling hand of developers and increased population with her charm still undiminished. We will find eulogies about her ranging from governors, soldiers, sailors, artists, great writers to ordinary citizens. She is eternally mercurial and a place of solace to those who pause to share her joys.

Some of my favourite pictures—mercifully reproduced in generous scale, are in this book.

Captain Arthur Phillip, first Governor of the colony of New South Wales, was greatly impressed by its harbour. It is, he wrote, 'the finest harbour in the world, in which a thousand sail of the line may ride in the most perfect security.' He chose a cove in the harbour which had a supply of fine spring water where 'ships can anchor so close to the shore that, at a very small expense, quays may be constructed at which the largest vessels may unload.' He called it 'Sydney Cove' in honour of Lord Sydney, Secretary of State for the Home Department. The harbour had already been named by Captain James Cook 'Port Jackson' after George Jackson, Judge-Advocate of the Fleet.

The early years of the colony were difficult and uncertain. Drought, disease, the restlessness of the convict settlers, overdue supply ships and crop failure prompted Phillip to write: 'No country offers less assistance to first settlers than this does.'

The struggle to get a foothold on the continent led early artists to focus on buildings and structures. In the drawings and prints of Watling, Eyre and Major Taylor we find clusters and rows of wattle and daub, stone and timber houses accurately and meticulously drawn. The relationship of each dwelling to the next is calculated with a fine mathematical precision that is a hallmark of some of the early topographical artists whose job it was to record officially the growth and development of the colony. In these pictures the harbour recedes in importance, appearing merely as a benign lake sheltering an assorted array of supply ships.

Thomas Watling, the colony's first professional artist, arrived in Sydney as a convict in 1792. The inaccurately titled *A Direct North General View of Sydney Cove* (it is in fact a *southern* view), attributed to Watling, is charmingly evasive in its description of the harbour, the flora and fauna and the topographical outlines of the settlement. This is one of the first paintings of the colony which deliberately or unconsciously distorts the facts.

The coming of Governor Macquarie on the last day of 1809 marked the beginning of a new era. Under his wise and sensitive leadership the colony grew from a prison into a settlement offering a sense of freedom which could not be found in England. Assisted by a convict architect of genius, Francis Greenway, Macquarie transformed Sydney from a humpy village to a town of elegance and refinement. Fine houses, public buildings and roads, many of which are Sydney's pride today, were constructed. An excellent Taylor shows this development. Hospitals, Government House stables (now the Conservatorium of Music), St James Church and orderly rows of tidy dwellings forcibly demonstrate how Macquarie, in one decade, changed the face of Sydney.

The following years saw the trebling of the population, the crossing of the Blue Mountains, the development of large agricultural estates and the beginning of the exploration and opening up of the continent. But the greatest and most momentous change occurred with the discovery of gold at Bathurst in February 1851. Almost overnight Sydney Harbour became a teeming traffic-way, with ships arriving daily, bringing with them adventurers from all parts of the world. The sleepy seaport, dotted with stone villas, churches and houses, now became a bustling, excited cosmopolitan centre.

Conrad Martens, who arrived in Sydney in 1835 and died there in 1878, encapsulates this bursting optimism. For the first time Sydney and the harbour are portrayed in proper scale and grandeur. Martens had a Turneresque breadth which allowed him to depict the dramatic effect of storm, cloud and sun which are so typical of the harbour. After the departure of Macquarie, Sydney had continued to develop into a city of substantial buildings and Martens' paintings reveal the urbanity, gentility and ease which characterized the city of his time.

Many lesser painters followed Martens' tradition, seeing the harbour as a place of ease, elegance and refinement. But it took Arthur Streeton, Roberts and Conder to democratize and individualize it. These artists saw instinctively that the harbour was a natural playground as well as a focus for the bohemian culturati of the city. Artists' camps sprang up around the foreshores and coves from the 1890s until the First World War. The paintings produced in this period reflect an astonishing quality of joy, freedom and youthful sensitivity which was eventually suffocated by the fierce brutality of the war. The post-war era was to produce something dramatically different.

Australia entered the machine age with an icon, the Sydney Harbour Bridge, which was quite as dramatic as the Eiffel Tower. Grace Cossington Smith's painting of the bridge two years before its completion gives the scene a religious aura. Less romantic, but just as striking, are Margaret Preston's sombre and mechanical woodcuts of the reaches of the harbour.

With the modern movement—to which de Maistre, Roland Wakelin, John D. Moore and Lloyd Rees all contributed differing visions—the harbour takes on a more complex intellectual and expressionistic scenario. Visions of the harbour after the Second World War become more menacing, self-conscious and angst-ridden. John Passmore's threatened bathers is a perfect example of this very different mood. Boyd, in a later work, views the harbour in much the same manner, portraying the houses perched on the foreshore as desperately fragile intruders into a primitive and wild world.

From the fifties to the seventies some of Australia's most talented artists have returned to the harbour for inspiration. Each brings a completely individualist approach—from Brett Whiteley to John Firth-Smith, from Shay Docking to Sidney Nolan. Perhaps my own works, which combine elements of optimism, cynicism and sin, have supplied yet another dimension to this magnetic and powerful theme. If Whiteley's views of the harbour have a luxuriant and fetid mood of South Pacific over-ripeness, Firth-Smith's, by contrast, present a formalism which dwells on the captives of the harbour itself—its ships and boats.

Sydney Harbour has provided artists from Australia and overseas with one of their most challenging images. For some it has been seen as a spectacle of grandeur, for others as an idyllic playground or as an image of escape and fantasy. A few have seen it as a paradise of progress. While the harbour itself has changed little, the visions of the harbour have been as numerous and diversified as the society which inhabits its foreshores.

John Olsen
Sydney
1979

A Direct North General View of Sydney Cove

A Direct North General View of Sydney Cove 1794
Oil. 88.2 × 129.5 cm
Dixson Galleries, Sydney

Thomas Watling *(b. 1762)*

Thomas Watling, the colony's first professional artist, arrived in Sydney as a convict in 1792, having been convicted of forging Bank of Scotland notes.

Like other Englishmen, Watling found the new colony unfriendly and forbidding, hot, fly-ridden and dusty, without one familiar plant, animal, tree or bird. The only oil painting attributed to him, however, gives no hint of this attitude. The legend on the back of the painting reads: *A Direct North General View of Sydney Cove the chief British Settlement in New South Wales as it appeared in 1794 being the seventh Year from its Establishment. Painted immediatly (sic) from Nature by T. Watling*. The painting is conceived in traditional eighteenth century classical landscape terms, and chooses to ignore the botanical facts, the unfamiliar spatial arena and the harsh, unkempt and ragged buildings of the colony.

The Sydney that Watling here presents is an idyllic Arcadia and the harbour a Georgian ornamental lake nestling against a luxuriant foreshore dappled with a few cottages and highlighted by the Governor's residence. The trees, too, are entirely exotic—decorative products of his imagination. So too is the scene of leisure and elegance. The image of two gentlemen strolling through the woods with a dog, pausing to chat on the dirt road at evening beneath a sky punctuated by a flock of graceful birds, is a civilized Englishman's dream.

If Watling's painting is a romantic vision of Sydney Cove, what then was the reality of life in the infant colony? In 1794 Sydney Cove was still an extensive gaol. Discipline was harsh; punishments, even for minor offences, were severe. For many years after the first settlement, walking in the 'Row' or street after dark without a passport or password was a punishable offence. Rum drinking and gambling were the two great recreations of the people and drunkenness was the order of the day and lightly regarded. Indeed, it was even officially condoned, for the owners of the grog shops cum gambling dens were frequently senior NCOs of the New South Wales Corps.

For the early colonists existence was a daily struggle and the environment was not conducive to merriment, nor did it relate to the leisured pace depicted in Watling's painting. However, given such a harsh reality, it is scarcely surprising that the artist preferred to produce a nostalgic replica of an English country scene.

Watling, however, was fully aware of his surroundings. He did in fact have a sensitivity to the harbour and its landscape. In 1792 he wrote to his aunt in Scotland about the 'majestic trees' and 'the sky clear and warm; in the summer very seldom overcast'. 'The easy, liberal mind,' he concluded, 'will be here filled with astonishment and find much entertainment from the various novel objects that every where present themselves.'

Watling was an accomplished landscape painter and an accurate zoological artist. Many of his watercolours and drawings of coastal landscapes, native birds, insects and plants are to be found in the British Natural History Museum.

View of Sydney from West Side of Cove 1806
Handcoloured aquatint. 34.5 × 64 cm
Mitchell Library, Sydney

John Eyre *(b. c 1771)*

John Eyre was born *c* 1771 and was a native of Coventry. At an early age he was apprenticed to his father, a woolcomber and weaver and it is to be presumed that he followed his father's trade. It is likely that in Coventry he took painting lessons from Joseph Barnes, for his work indicates a certain degree of professional training and is closely akin to the English topographical school of drawing.

In 1799, when he was twenty-eight, Eyre was convicted of housebreaking and transported to Australia aboard the convict ship *Canada* which arrived at Sydney Cove in December 1801. Very little is known of his life in Sydney, although he advertised for a box of water-colours in the *Sydney Gazette* in 1804, and there is a reference to his employment to paint numbers on the houses of Sydney at the rate of sixpence per house—to be paid from the Police Fund. He spent only eleven years in the colony before returning to Europe as a free man, but in that time he made a lasting contribution to Australian art, providing many paintings, engravings and panoramic views of Sydney.

Although at this time the settlement still largely resembled a camp, there were many substantial houses and administrative buildings, and Eyre's Sydney as depicted in *View of Sydney from West Side of Cove*, has an appearance of permanence. White settlers seldom appear in his pictures and local flora and fauna receive only scant attention. Houses and buildings were his chief interest. He was a master of detail; his houses, executed with infinite care were printed in a single colour and hand-tinted to produce a more appealing effect. His drawings are precise but simple and there is no attempt to romanticize the landscape.

In 1810 two of Eyre's views of Sydney Cove were exhibited in London and in 1811 four of his works appeared as illustrations for *The Present Picture of New South Wales* by David Dickenson Mann. Following his departure from the colony, more of his works appeared in Absalom West's *Views of New South Wales* which was the first publication of its kind in the colony.

Typical of Eyre's work is this hand-coloured aquatint, a view of the Sydney Rocks area, looking across Circular Quay to Bennelong Point where the Opera House now stands. As in many of his paintings, heavy rocks dominate the foreground. In the middle ground, a group of Aborigines appears to be living naturally, close to the settlement, while in the distance one can recognize the flour mill, a well-known landmark of the time.

Major James Taylor *(d. 1829)*

Views of Sydney 1823
1 The Entrance of Port Jackson and part of the Town of Sydney in New South Wales
Handcoloured aquatint. 47.8 × 65 cm
2 The Town of Sydney in New South Wales
Handcoloured aquatint. 47.5 × 64.5 cm
3 Part of the Harbour of Port Jackson and the country between Sydney and the Blue Mountains, New South Wales
Handcoloured aquatint. 47.5 × 64.5 cm
Handcoloured aquatints by Robert Havell and Sons, from the drawings by James Taylor
Rex Nan Kivell Collection, National Library of Australia

Probably born between 1780 and 1790 in England, Major James Taylor joined the British Army in 1804 and arrived in Sydney with the Northamptonshire Regiment in 1817 as a military artist and topographer. He remained in the colony only six years. Taylor, like Eyre, was one of the main exponents of the Australian topographical school of drawing.

In 1817 New South Wales was still mainly a convict settlement with sixteen thousand convicts, the same number of ex-convicts and only seven thousand free settlers. By this time, however, the harbour had become civilized. Because of the desperate need for grazing land, large areas of the foreshores had been given over to grazing cattle and sheep.

Taylor's panoramic *Views of Sydney* is an early presentation of Sydney in terms of real estate. This aquatint, which was published in three parts, was designed to show the topographical, social and economic aspects of the colony. The centre section depicts the Military Hospital designed by John Watts which still stands on Observatory Hill. In the total picture Taylor gives a sweeping view, from east to west, of the existing settlement and outlying areas around the harbour. Social progress is demonstrated by the officers strolling in the garden of the hospital, Aborigines bizarrely dressed in togas like ancient Romans, borders of English flowers, and manicured lawns. These are all contrasted with views, further afield, of naked Aborigines, native flora, and the monotonous bush in the background.

The intricacy of detail challenges the viewer to inspect the work as one would a series of incidents. It is a picture of charming, perhaps naive, social comment. The everyday activities of the colony are suggested by the men quarrying stone, grooming horses, cutting wood and herding cattle.

The harbour in Taylor's picture is placid, but it is also endowed with a great amplitude of scale. The sky, which takes up three-quarters of the picture, has a dimension which was to be fully realized only much later by the Heidelberg School in the late nineteenth century.

Views of Sydney

Views of Sydney

Port Jackson from Dawes' Battery

Port Jackson from Dawes' Battery
c 1842
Canvas mounted on board. 50.5 × 67 cm
Mitchell Library, Sydney

John Skinner Prout *(1806–1876)*

Born in England in 1806, John Skinner Prout migrated to Australia in 1840. The view of Port Jackson after the long months at sea appears to have made a profound and lasting impression on Prout; for him there was no harbour in the world 'more beautiful, extensive and commodious' than Sydney Harbour.

Prout spent eight years in the colonies of New South Wales and Tasmania and exerted a lively influence upon the local art world. He stimulated much interest in painting by giving popular lectures at the Sydney Mechanics Institute soon after his arrival in 1840. He wrote enthusiastic discourses on the countryside, its vegetation, harbours and inlets. With his own lithographic press he published three books dealing with Australian scenes. He had an extensive knowledge of every aspect of Port Jackson—its varying depths, the names of the coves and their derivations, the navigational aspects of the inlets and channels. His works display a developed understanding of the picturesque details of particular places, rather than an emphasis on topographical accuracy alone.

Originally a topographer, Prout, while in Australia, developed a freer style which influenced other artists of the colony, probably including Conrad Martens. On his return to England, however, he reverted to topographical work when he used large numbers of his drawings from New South Wales and Tasmania to create dioramas of Australia. Prout presented these with accompanying lectures and appropriate music. Apparently they were of great interest in England, especially to prospective migrants.

Prout painted *Port Jackson from Dawes' Battery* in the doorway of Colonel Barney's residence in the Battery at Dawes Point, looking east towards the lighthouse. The foreground forms a stage for three red-coated sentinels, some field pieces and a cannon. The relaxed position of the soldiers is, perhaps, intended to suggest that the colony's defences were more for show than for action. The cattle and the group at the water's edge help to create an impression of quiet inactivity, while the serene space of the harbour stretching in the distance gives the entire scene an almost dream-like quality.

View of Darlinghurst, Woolloomooloo Bay on Left

Conrad Martens *(1801–1878)*

View of Darlinghurst, Woolloomooloo Bay on Left 1843
Oil on canvas. 46.5 × 65 cm
Collection: James Fairfax

Elizabeth Bay and Elizabeth Bay House 1839
Watercolour. 45.8 × 64.8 cm
Felton Bequest 1950
National Gallery of Victoria

View from Neutral Bay—Breaking of the Storm 1850
Watercolour. 45.1 × 65.4 cm
Private collection

Born in England in 1801, the son of a German-born consul for Austria in London, Conrad Martens studied painting under Copley Fielding in London. In 1832, after embarking on a voyage to India aboard the *Hyacinth*, he transferred to another ship, the *Beagle* when he heard that it wished to employ an artist. On the *Beagle* he formed a close friendship with Charles Darwin and was greatly influenced by this imaginative scientist. From the Commander of the *Beagle*, Captain FitzRoy, he acquired a sense of precision in the observation of atmospheric conditions, cloud formations and the eccentricities of the weather.

Martens' great ability to judge atmospheric colour owes much to his years on the *Beagle*. Although in 1835 he was still painting in the topographical tradition he gradually freed his style from the restrictions of this tradition without ever losing the precision of drawing. In 1851 he wrote of the necessity of preserving the character and true delineation of the trees and plants in the landscapes of this country, a point which he considered of great consequence so long as it did not amount to absolute servility.

On his arrival in Australia Martens settled in the Rocks area where he set up a studio and conducted classes which would certainly have been the most sophisticated in the colony. However, only a precarious living could be earned in the colony from painting and lecturing. In 1863 Martens was appointed Assistant Parliamentary Librarian in New South Wales, a secure post which allowed him time to paint and which gave him an assured income until his death in 1878.

While Martens' work covers a wide range of subjects, it was undoubtedly Sydney Harbour that most fascinated him. Though Martens could not match the genius of Turner, several of his watercolours of Sydney Harbour can be said to equal those of Turner in the dramatic effect which is achieved by the use of light.

While many consider *View from Neutral Bay—Breaking of the Storm* to be Martens' finest work—and certainly, in theatrical terms, it is his most ambitious—*Elizabeth Bay and Elizabeth Bay House* must rival it for sheer poetic beauty. In both paintings the artist has taken a high panoramic perspective with the land masses in the foreground serving as a frame for the splendid play of light issuing from the heavens.

View of Darlinghurst, Woolloomooloo Bay on Left is one of Martens' most elegant works. Here he presents a view of the harbour seen from one of the grand villas that dotted the shoreline. In the foreground an artfully arranged still life suggests the princely lifestyle of the occupant whose residence, which is unseen, commands this view.

Of all the artists who painted Sydney Harbour, Conrad Martens was its most passionate and professional devotee. In watercolour after watercolour he imbued its expanse of water, its shorelines and atmospheric effects with a beauty and dramatic grandeur that no other artist has ever achieved.

Elizabeth Bay and Elizabeth Bay House

View from Neutral Bay — Breaking of the Storm

Sydney Heads

Sydney Heads 1865
Oil on canvas. 56 × 94 cm
Bequest of Major A. W. Hall 1974
Art Gallery of New South Wales

Eugen von Guerard *(1811–1901)*

Eugen von Guerard was the son of the Viennese Court Painter to Emperor Franz I. Born in Vienna in 1811, he came to Australia in 1852 in search of gold and spent sixteen unprofitable months on the Ballarat goldfields. During this time, as is obvious from his journal, he was closely observing the countryside. On 14 August 1854, he wrote of a sheep station which he observed on a walk to the Bald Hills, not far from Ballarat: '. . . green fields, fences, shepherds' huts, and the squatter's house with a pretty garden . . . The hills, . . . are three to four hundred feet in height, and are most certainly of volcanic origin. The view from the top is grand . . . The forests through which we went are magnificent, the wattle in full bloom.'

After his marriage, in Melbourne, he began to travel throughout Australia, painting scenes which impressed him sufficiently. Von Guerard was always seeking the 'grand vista', the sublime scene capable of elevating the spirit and paying homage to the great Creator. Sydney Harbour, with its panoramic views, jutting rocks and endless moods, was a natural subject for him.

He was most impressed by that 'small aperture', the entrance to the Harbour. But, characteristically, he places that entrance in a broad perspective as if the artist and the viewer are standing on an imaginary platform and looking down upon the scene.

By the time *Sydney Heads* was executed, the colony had begun to spread right round the shores of the harbour. Watson's Bay, near the imposing South Head, was a rural village. A few dirt roads led to the scattered fishermen's huts and boatsheds and to the cove where sailing boats lay peacefully at anchor.

The painting is evenly and harmoniously divided into three horizontal bands—earth, water and sky. The foreground provides a picturesque cross-section of the community—a man with a fishing pole, accompanied by his dog, a group of labourers around a fire and a horse-drawn buggy in which sit a well-dressed upper class couple.

Despite these human vignettes and the close attention that von Guerard gives to the rendering of rocks, plants, grasses and trees, the artist's intentions are quite clear. He wants the viewer to revel in the sense of space, to admire the great calm and silent stretches of water and to feel the wonder of Nature.

Sydney Harbour Looking Towards Sydney 1848
Oil. 73 × 97.5 cm
Mitchell Library, Sydney

Jacob Janssen *(1779–1856)*

Little is known about Jacob Janssen. Like some other artists in the early days of the colony, he was a painter-adventurer who had travelled extensively. Prior to his arrival in Sydney from Manila on the *Louisa Campbell* on 5 December 1840, he is known to have visited the United States of America, South America, Singapore and India. Janssen was born in Elbing, Prussia, in 1779. There are several references to the excellence of his miniatures, but Janssen also excelled in landscape and still life. He exhibited pictures in Sydney in 1847 and 1849, and died there in 1856.

Janssen's *Sydney Harbour* looking towards Sydney from New South Head Road is both elegant and decorative. Obviously enchanted by the tall-tufted gum tree, Janssen places a white eucalyptus on the left-hand side of his picture under which sit two labourers engrossed in conversation over lunch. On the dirt road, which stretches across the foreground like a brown ribbon, is a colonial gentleman out in a horse-chaise with his lady companion. Obviously the chaise, the high-stepping chestnut, and the whippet running beside his master's carriage are objects to admire.

The harbourscape, sprinkled with villas, surrounded by wooded coves and punctuated with small islands, is calm and serene. The sky, untrammelled by any threatening clouds, reflects the tranquil mood of a country scene.

It is interesting that Janssen lets the harbour dominate his figures. The open reaches of water, despite the comforting land masses that protectively frame the edge of the painting, spatially reduce the humans to toy-like figures. Janssen, even as a decorative painter, imparts to the viewer the sense that human life in the 1840s was indeed a tenuous and vulnerable experience.

To a newcomer, the bustling city could seem familiar, thoroughly English and even gracious. However, to the most casual observer, it would be obvious that the city was isolated. Even a decade later some of the exotic quality of the city had vanished. Frank Fowler noted in 1858 that: 'To talk now of flocks of parrots alighting on the trees about Sydney would be like talking of wolves prowling about the city of London.'

The charm of Janssen's picture is that it captures an almost naive sense of Sydney and its harbour in 1848.

Sydney Harbour Looking Towards Sydney

Picnic at Mrs Macquarie's Chair 1855
Oil. 63.5 × 91.5 cm
Dixson Galleries, Sydney

Unknown Artist

The identity of the artist of *Picnic at Mrs Macquarie's Chair* is still uncertain, although present opinion tentatively attributes the painting to F. C. Terry, an artist who died in 1869. Others whose names have been suggested are Edward Roper, J. B. Henderson, Jacob Janssen, E. Thomas, O. W. Brierly and S. T. Gill. The costume of the figures in the painting suggest its date as *c* 1855.

The inclusion of the painting in this book provides a social dimension to the harbour theme. Like S. T. Gill, the 'Picnic' Artist displays an interest in social manners, behaviour and dress; but, unlike Gill, he is also interested in landscape and atmospheric surroundings. It is of interest that, rather than an exotic or fanciful location for his scene, he has chosen a popular recreation spot—Lady Macquarie's Chair (recently correctly renamed Mrs Macquarie's Chair).

In the words of Mrs Charles Meredith, Mrs Macquarie, wife of the Governor of the colony of New South Wales 'had this Domain laid out after her own plans; walks and drives were cut through the rocks and shrubs . . . On the high point of the promontory some large horizontal rocks have been slightly assisted by art into the form of a great seat or throne called Lady Macquarie's Chair, above which an inscription informs the visitor to whose excellent taste and benevolent feeling he is indebted for the improvement of this lovely spot.'

The Picnic Artist presents a gay, rollicking view of men, women and children, dogs and crisply pitched tents spread beneath the natural sandstone 'Chair' which is carved into the jutting promontory. It is a happy and sunny scene—a Sunday outing where people, dressed in their best clothes, are eating, drinking and enjoying themselves along the foreshores of the harbour. The artist places special emphasis on the jutting overhang of the rocks, realistically showing the inscription chiselled into the back of the seat and deploying his figures beneath its weighty shadow with the eye of a natural observer of both man and landscape.

To the modern viewer, the scene has some endearingly primitive features—the overbalancing of the composition to the right and the somewhat awkward posturing of the figures. On the whole, however, the painting is remarkable for its masterly and confident handling of a panoramic scene which is filled with so many figures, anecdotal details, landscape and sea forms.

Picnic at Mrs Macquarie's Chair

General View of Sydney From the North Shore 1861
Watercolour. 37.5 × 72 cm
Dixson Galleries, Sydney

S. T. Gill *(1818–1880)*

Samuel Thomas Gill was born in England in 1818 and arrived in Australia in 1839. He is best known for his illustrative interpretations of the ribald life on the goldfields and for his drawings of miners, country squires and autocratic and dissolute squatters. Although he studied with his father, an artist, he was largely self-taught.

In 1849 a set of Gill's lithographs of well-known colonists, *Heads of People*, was published and, in 1856, a set of lithographs entitled *Scenery in and around Sydney* was also published. Gill's first sketches of the goldfields appeared in 1852 under the title *A Series of Sketches of the Victorian Gold Diggings as they are*. Further sets followed in the next sixteen years.

Gill was employed by newspapers and journals —principally the *Victoria Illustrated* and Melbourne *Punch*—in a capacity similar to that of the newspaper photographer of today. He was a talented and honest reporter of the sights and incidents which he portrayed, although he was on one occasion involved in a lawsuit over the inaccurate reporting of a horse race.

This view of Sydney Harbour, entitled *General View of Sydney from the North Shore*, is an honest one, neither romanticized nor idealized. It shows a new area of land being opened up on the northern shore, as primitively pegged as a goldmining lease or a modern subdivision. There are no acres of lush foliage, tropical birds, sparkling villas or English gardens; it is, rather, a rough colonial frontier complete with dust, stumps, stubborn bullocks and barren ground waiting to be developed.

Gill's last sketch was one entitled *Dust Storm in Elizabeth Street*. He had by this time become an alcoholic and a derelict, one of a group of hopeless men who frequented the steps of the Elizabeth Street Post Office. He died in the street and was buried in a pauper's grave. Later the Historical Society of Victoria erected a headstone to his memory at Melbourne General Cemetery.

General View of Sydney From the North Shore

Beach and Timber Mill—Berry's Bay, Sydney

Arthur Streeton *(1867–1943)*

Night Scene c 1890
Oil on panel. 21.5 × 68.5 cm
Private collection

Circular Quay c 1893
Oil on cedar panel. 19.8 × 47.7 cm
Australian National Gallery, Canberra

McMahon's Point 1890
Oil on panel. 44 × 30.5 cm
Hinton Collection. Armidale College of Advanced Education and the Council of the City of Armidale

Sirius Cove 1892
Oil on panel. 29 × 21.5 cm
Hinton Collection. Armidale College of Advanced Education and the Council of the City of Armidale

Untitled Harbour Painting 1881
Oil on wood panel. 13.5 × 23.4 cm
Australian National Gallery, Canberra

The Wharf, Mosman's Bay c 1895
Oil on panel. 17.5 × 64 cm
Hinton Collection. Armidale College of Advanced Education and the Council of the City of Armidale

After studying at the Melbourne National Gallery School under Folingsby, Arthur Streeton, at the age of twenty was introduced to the Box Hill artists' camp where he met Tom Roberts, Frederick McCubbin, Louis Abrahams and Charles Conder. Together, these artists established the distinctive national art style referred to as the 'Heidelberg School'. Streeton and Roberts later moved to Sydney where they founded the Sirius Cove camps. These and other camps continued to dot the shorelines of Sydney Harbour until the outbreak of World War I.

Artists chose to live in such camps for a variety of reasons, not the least of which were that they provided an open and free lifestyle and were cheaper, and certainly more entertaining, than most boarding houses. For a pound a week an artist could enjoy breathtaking views of the harbour, be close to the rocky natural bushland and have easy access to the city. Many of Streeton's works were painted around this camp area of Sirius Cove.

The painting *Night Scene* (1890) captures in paint the romantically evocative mood of a letter written by Streeton to his friend, Tom Roberts: 'I lay on the paddlebox coming home from Manly last night, and the soft, dark breath of the harbour playing through my hair . . . All seemed a dream . . . Just like a long, sad, soothing melody.' The picture has an immediacy that is rare even in Streeton's work. In it, Streeton gives a new dimension to the image of the harbour—the harbour as a playground. His vision is unquestionably that of a hedonist, a poet and a sensualist.

In *Sirius Cove* (1892) Streeton gives the spectator a frontal view of the cove. The artist has skilfully constructed a strong composition of interlocking right angles and horizontals. The bush, the rock and the water are painted in glowing tones of yellow, russet and brown, with enchanting bluish-pink highlights. The steps leading to the top of the cove become a decorative zig-zag, a compositional device which unites the water and the land. The overall mood of the painting is more sombre and reflective than is usual in Streeton's work.

McMahons Point (1890) is a view of the harbour from a residential vantage point. On the left the focal point is the roof of a house, to the right of which a child, in a sailor suit and straw hat, ascends a steep dirt path. Beside the wharf below, a steam paddleboat with smoke curling into the grey-blue sky, waits to take on a few passengers. One feels very much the presence of the painter, seated at the top of the hill behind the house swiftly sketching with small brush strokes the scene below him.

In contrast to this very intimate picture is the panoramic *Circular Quay* (1893). This is not a painting about the pleasures of artists' camps and discreet coves and boatsheds. This is Streeton, the artist, paying homage to Sydney itself. He has used a strong diagonal and 'L' shape to harness the various components of the scene—the ferries, commercial vessels, steamboats, and crowds of moving people. Perhaps the most compelling feature of this work is Streeton's extraordinary ability to suggest so successfully all the dynamic vitality of a great port.

McMahon's Point

Sirius Cove

Untitled Harbour Painting

The Wharf, Mosman's Bay

The Camp, Sirius Cove c 1889–99

Tom Roberts *(1856–1931)*

The Camp, Sirius Cove c 1889–09
Oil on canvas on pulpboard. 25.4 × 34.6 cm
Art Gallery of New South Wales

Circular Quay 1898
Oil on wood panel. 9 × 19.7 cm
Private collection

Mosman's Bay 1894
Oil. 68.9 × 94.9 cm
Hinton Collection. Armidale College of Advanced Education and the Council of the City of Armidale

Tom Roberts was born in Dorchester, England, in 1856 and arrived in Australia with his family at the age of thirteen following the death of his father. Roberts might have made a brilliant politician or become a powerful captain of industry. Instead he was to become the founder of the first indigenous school of Australian painting.

His first job was with a local photographer in Collingwood, Victoria. He later worked at the National Gallery School under Louis Buvelot and Thomas Clark. Clark was impressed by Roberts' talent, toughness and tenacity and urged him to go to England. After four years in Europe, during which time he met and was influenced by Whistler, he returned to Melbourne in 1885.

With Frederick McCubbin and Louis Abrahams, Roberts set up the first artists' camps at Box Hill and Heidelberg where they were later joined by Charles Conder and Arthur Streeton. In these camps Australian Impressionism was born.

In a letter to the editor of the *Argus* on 30 August 1889, the 'impressionists' stated the principles on which they worked: '. . . we will not be led by any forms of composition or light and shade; . . . any effect of nature which moves us strongly by its beauty, whether strong or vague in its drawing, defined or indefinite in its light, rare or ordinary in colour, is worthy of our best efforts and of the love of those who love our art. . . . we will do our best to put only the truth down, and only as much as we feel sure of seeing.'

In 1891 Roberts and Streeton went to Sydney and camped near Saunders' Boat House, Mosman Bay. *Mosman's Bay* has the same deep diagonal space formed by the wharf as has Conder's *Departure of the Orient*. The scene, however, is viewed from a closer point than Conder's picture. In the foreground a young couple is out boating. She carries a red parasol whose colour is repeated in the crimson dresses of the figures on the shore. The cove, with its deep dark green reflecting water, is handsomely framed by the strong promenade and the loosely painted bush rising from the waterfront.

The Camp, Sirius Cove is a more objective picture. Here the artist is not interested in the panoramic view of the harbour and its bustling activities. As in *Circular Quay*, the scene is a secluded cove in which a lone sailing boat is anchored, surrounded by autumnal bush which is reflected in a golden-blue strip of water. While the quality of the work is texturally vibrant, the composition is photographically informal. In *Circular Quay*, painted in 1898, Roberts is concerned with a more precise description of streets and buildings.

Roberts' Sydney period is much more relaxed and carefree in quality than some of the later works in which he eulogizes the muscular quality of the bush.

Circular Quay

Mosman's Bay

Sydney Harbour Ferry 1893
Oil. 43 × 32 cm
Hinton Collection. Armidale College of Advanced Education and the Council of the City of Armidale

Albert Fullwood *(1863–1930)*

Albert Fullwood is possibly one of Australia's most neglected, if not forgotten, artists. He was born in England in 1863. On his arrival in Sydney in 1881, at the age of eighteen, he found employment as an illustrator.

His first works, which were landscapes, were shown in the 1882 annual exhibition of the Art Society of New South Wales. In the eighties, under the influence of Livingstone Hopkins ('Hop'), many artists, including Fullwood, began 'taking up' etching. This was ultimately the area in which Fullwood was to have the most success.

The economic situation in Australia after the bank crash of 1893 forced Fullwood to seek better opportunities overseas. For twelve months he lived in America, after which he moved to London, where his financial situation immediately improved. In 1902 he had a successful exhibition which was followed by three more one-man shows. Fullwood's talent became so well recognized that he was soon having exhibitions in Paris, Berlin and Dresden.

When the First World War began, Fullwood, then over fifty, joined a number of artists, actors and musicians in the Allied Art Corps which trained at Earl's Court. Fullwood was placed on non-combat duty in the Royal Army Medical Corps for two years. At the beginning of 1918, he was commissioned to go to the front to paint for the Australian War Museum.

In 1920 Fullwood returned to Australia and held exhibitions in Melbourne and Sydney. In one of those twists of reasoning which characterize the bureaucratic mind, Fullwood who had, when he was overseas, always been considered an Australian painter, was declared by the Customs Department to be English. He was therefore taxed on all the paintings he brought from England. Because of this tariff on his paintings Fullwood returned to England.

Fullwood's *Sydney Harbour Ferry* (1893), despite its sombre mood, has a spontaneous brusqueness and displays a sensuous handling of oil paint and a quickened emotional pace which is unusual in paintings of its time. Here, the viewer is confronted with an abrupt mental image of a passing moment and a pervasive romantic lyricism.

Sydney Harbour Ferry

Sydney Harbour 1908
Oil on panel. 25.4 × 35.5 cm
Australian National Gallery, Canberra

Carrick Fox *(1876–1952)*

Ethel Carrick Fox was born in England *c* 1876 and died in Melbourne in 1952. As an artist she has always been overshadowed by her husband, E. Phillips Fox, whom she married as a student at the Slade School, London, in 1905. Following their marriage the couple toured Europe and eventually settled in Paris, which became a magnet for Carrick Fox throughout her life.

In 1908, Carrick Fox made her first visit to Australia with her husband, an Australian by birth, and during this visit she completed this charming 'very French' painting of Sydney Harbour. After a short time in Australia they were irresistibly drawn back to Paris, but at the outbreak of the First World War they returned once more to Australia where Phillips Fox died in 1915. When the war ended, Carrick went to India and then to Europe, but the Second World War found her again in Australia, promoting French artists and organizing projects to aid Australian artists stranded in Europe during the Occupation.

Carrick Fox's *Sydney Harbour* is, in its general mood, reminiscent of the sub-Impressionist paintings of the French artist Vuillard whose works often capture the same regatta-like gaiety. Using a brisk sketchy impressionist technique, the artist has depicted a group of pretty, fashion-conscious ladies promenading on a city quay. The women, grouped in a chatty, informal composition, wear tea-gowns, tray-size hats and carry umbrellas. The predominance of white billowing dresses gives the scene an innocent and youthful air.

The harbour, in Carrick Fox's hands, has become an intimate French port, with the city skyline acting as an indistinct romantic backdrop. Throughout the picture there is a feeling of snapping summer breezes and cheerful activity. For Carrick Fox (as for Streeton) the Harbour is a playground, a place of spectacle and pleasure.

Sydney Harbour

Departure of the Orient—Circular Quay
1888
Oil on canvas. 45.1 × 50.1 cm
Art Gallery of New South Wales

Charles Conder *(1868–1909)*

Charles Conder was born in England in 1868. In his early teens he was sent by his father to Sydney to work with his uncle as an apprentice surveyor in the Lands Department of New South Wales.

Against family pressure Conder abandoned this career and joined an architectural firm as a lithographic apprentice. He soon became an illustrator and his weekly drawings signed 'E.E.' appeared in the *Illustrated Sydney News*. He attended the Art Society School drawing classes conducted by Julian Ashton and night painting classes with A. J. Daplyn. Later, he studied at the Melbourne National Gallery School under McCubbin, and then in Paris.

Departure of the Orient—Circular Quay, painted when Conder was barely twenty, reflects the influence of Nerli, Whistler and Tom Roberts. It was Conder's first successful painting and was purchased for the Art Gallery of New South Wales. Like Nerli's *Street Scene on a Rainy Night*, painted in the same year (1888), Conder's picture shows the Quay on a wet overcast day. The greys of the sky merge with the slate-coloured water. Light reflections are enlivened by the mingling crowd about the dock. The subtle atmospheric effects are dramatized by a strong diagonal movement. The sharp right-angle of the wharf is repeated in the shapes of the warehouses and the angles of the boats. Conder adds picturesque detail in the images of a woman holding her skirt as she dashes through the rain, a vendor striding with a tray on his head, and the playful smoke of the ships.

When the novelist Joseph Conrad visited Sydney in 1880 he remarked that the comings and goings of ships were an integral and colourful part of the life of Sydney residents. For them, the ships were running links with home, the carriers of news, the bearers of exciting cargo and the conveyors of new settlers. He wrote of Circular Quay that it was 'the integral part of one of the finest, most beautiful, vast, and safe bays the sun ever shone upon.' Conder's picture expresses these ideas on canvas.

After his success in Sydney, Conder went to Melbourne where he joined McCubbin and Streeton at the Box Hill artists' camp. This move linked his name permanently with the founders of the Australian Impressionist School —the Heidelberg Group. In 1890 Conder returned to England and died there in 1909. He had spent only seven years in Australia, but those years had ensured for him a place in the history of Australian art.

Waterfront, Sydney Harbour

Morning Glitter

Morning Glitter 1923
Oil on canvas. 51 × 61 cm
Sinclair Gillies Bequest
Art Gallery of New South Wales

Will Ashton *(1881–1963)*

Will Ashton was born in England in 1881 and came to Australia with his family at an early age. He studied with his father, James Ashton, who was teacher of drawing at Prince Alfred College, Adelaide. He then furthered his studies in England and France. From his father and from the famous marine artist, Julius Olsson, with whom he studied in Cornwall, Ashton acquired a strong love of the water. Many of his paintings are water scenes. He said: 'Water is alive and I dislike static things. Bridges, barges, rivers, the sea, people and streets are my favourite subjects and it is said that we paint best the things we love.'

By 1907 Ashton had established a reputation as a painter of picturesque European subjects. For many years he travelled between Europe and Australia and held successful exhibitions in Australian capital cities.

Ashton was a fierce conservative and vehemently and vocally opposed the modern movement in Australian art. He was Director of the Art Gallery of New South Wales from 1937 to 1944 and Chairman of the Commonwealth Art Advisory Board. He was knighted in 1960.

While paintings such as Nerli's *Berry's Bay* foreshadow the possible commercial exploitation that would eventually strangle and pollute the waters of the inner harbour, Will Ashton's painting, *Morning Glitter*, expresses the inevitability of that exploitation.

Despite the name which Ashton has given to his work, Darling Harbour is seen smothered in the blue haze of the smoke and smog of an inner industrial suburb. The crisp delineation of the foreshores, coves and inlets of colonial painters has given way to a confusion of factories, slums and warehouses.

The romanticizing of industrial horror has many precedents, among them Monet's soot-filled *La Gare Saint-Lazare* and Whistler's views of London's debris-ridden Thames.

Down the Hills to Berry's Bay

Roland Wakelin *(1887–1971)*

Down the Hills to Berry's Bay 1916
Oil on canvas. 68 × 122 cm
Art Gallery of New South Wales

The Fruit Seller, Farm Cove 1915
Oil on canvas on hardboard. 91.6 × 116.1 cm
Australian National Gallery, Canberra

Regatta
Oil on pulpboard. 86.5 × 112 cm
Australian National Gallery, Canberra

Born in Wellington, New Zealand, in 1887, Roland Wakelin arrived in Sydney in the summer of 1912. He studied with Dattilo Rubbo at the Royal Art Society School.

He worked as a commercial artist for a large part of his life—until a few years after the Second World War. Part of this time, from 1917 to 1922, was spent in the commercial art firm of Smith & Julius where he worked with such men as Sydney Ure Smith, Percy Leason, Lloyd Rees and Roy de Maistre. Wakelin was particularly interested in de Maistre's theory of colour notation and in 1919 they held their now famous exhibition of 'Colour Music' paintings.

Although his early art training was based on the academic tradition, Wakelin became interested in Impressionist techniques while studying under Rubbo. When the artist Nora Simpson returned from Europe with a book on Paul Cézanne Wakelin was deeply impressed by the reproductions of Cezanne's works. In Cézanne Wakelin saw for the first time an art that was bald, at times even clumsy, and exciting in its geometric simplicity. Wakelin immediately saw that this was the avenue he wanted to investigate. Lloyd Rees, in his book of reminiscences about Australian art and artists, *The Small Treasures of a Lifetime*, says he often felt there was a strange affinity between Wakelin and Cézanne: 'Both were retiring by nature and likely to shun company unless it was congenial to them. They also shared another quality in their drawing, painting, and writing—the elimination of the non-essential.' Wakelin was further enthused when, on a trip to England in 1922, he saw exhibitions of the works of Van Gogh and Cézanne.

After his London period Wakelin gradually emerged into full bloom as a Romantic artist. His pigment was rich, his brushstroke strong and his compositions extremely subtle.

Lloyd Rees writes that 'Sydney exerted a spell on the artist from the first moment, and he has often told me that when he first entered Sydney Heads he was filled with a desire to live and work there.'

This enthusiasm for Sydney landscape and harbour is reflected in the paintings *Down the Hills to Berry's Bay*, *The Fruit Seller*, *Farm Cove*, and *Regatta*.

Wakelin's *Regatta* foreshadows a sportsman's delight in the harbour, which would later be taken up by a contemporary Sydney painter, John Firth-Smith.

The Fruit Seller, Farm Cove

Regatta

The Harbour from McMahon's Point

The Harbour from McMahon's Point 1950
Oil on canvas. 77.1 × 99 cm
Art Gallery of New South Wales

The Blue Bay c 1938–45
Oil on canvas. 49.4 × 62 cm
Art Gallery of New South Wales

Looking East—Sundown 1978
Oil on canvas. 84 × 145 cm
Collection: Mrs A. I. McClelland

Lloyd Rees *(b. 1895)*

Born in Brisbane in 1895, Lloyd Rees came to Sydney at the age of twenty-one. He later described his first glimpse of Sydney Harbour as 'opal blue water, a band of golden sand, another of olive green trees; above them a skyline of coral pink shimmering against the limpid air . . . In that first long look Sydney cast her spell . . .'

After this first visit Rees returned to Brisbane. In 1917 he came to Sydney at the invitation of Sydney Ure Smith, to work in the commercial art firm of Smith & Julius.

From the beginning Rees was an enthusiastic devotee, not only of Sydney Harbour, but also of the city's architecture. His focus on the harbour, however, did not alter and he continued to paint its headlands, shores and bays, particularly McMahons Point where he lived for some years.

A visit to Europe in 1923 enabled Rees to study in Rome and London. The landscapes of Italy made a lasting impression on his work. Rees saw Sydney, with its domes and spires, as an almost Venetian scene—not as the sunless canyons of glass and steel we see today.

Rees himself says of these influences: '. . . of one thing I feel reasonably certain: whatever the influences, the artist must forget them when he starts to paint. Indeed, I hold strongly to the view that once a picture has come to life it dictates the terms of its own creation.'

While most artists saw the harbour as an arena of open space, Rees saw it as enclosed. In *The Harbour from McMahon's Point* he reinforces this feeling of enclosure. The warm undulating curves of the inlets and bays, and the landscape, painted in lead reds and olive greens, punctuated with rooftops and buildings become topographical points of reference. A curving road plunges the viewer's eye deeply into the harbour space, while the artist himself takes a more lofty viewpoint.

Looking East—Sundown, a late work, has a golden luminous glow which beautifully captures the harbour's mood moments before the sun disappears in the west. The streaks of burnt copper strike a beach, the wake of a ship, and are then echoed in the land mass in the distance. The scene, dissolved in light, holds the panoramic view in an iridescent radiance which is reminiscent of such later works of Claude Monet as *Rouen Cathedral* and *The Haystacks*.

Overall, Rees' vision of the harbour is classically romantic—the *temps perdu* of an architectural paradise lost.

The Blue Bay

Looking East—Sundown

The Bridge In-Curve 1930
Oil on pulpboard. 83.8 × 111.8 cm
National Gallery of Victoria

Grace Cossington Smith *(b. 1892)*

Born in 1892, Grace Cossington Smith studied in Sydney, England and Germany and became one of the leaders of the post-Impressionist movement in New South Wales. Her first exposure to the works of artists like Cézanne, Braque or Matisse seems to have come from looking at prints and reproductions in books, and it was not until 1950, on her second trip to Europe, that she saw her first original painting by Cézanne.

Her first 'one-man' exhibition was held in 1928. In an article in *Art in Australia* published the same year, Roland Wakelin wrote of her innovative role in the development of modern painting.

Cossington Smith has worked mainly in the seclusion of her Sydney northern suburbs home where she has lived since 1913.

The Sydney Harbour Bridge was one of the greatest engineering feats in Australia. The problem of spanning so vast a distance—almost a kilometre—had attracted engineers and architects since the idea was first proposed by Francis Greenway in 1815. When the bridge was completed in 1932, its effect on the residents of the city was immediate; their lives were at once expanded as the boundaries of the harbour were extended and linked. The curved steel gateway changed Sydney from a town to a grand city.

Artists, like everyone else, were delighted as they watched the construction and saw the two great arms of the growing bridge move closer together and finally meet. Grace Cossington Smith was one who took particular interest in the construction for, although a quiet and introspective person, she was a keen observer of the social and political events of the day. *The Bridge In-Curve* captures the excitement and enthusiasm which the sight of the rising bridge aroused in Sydney residents. We are engulfed in a sense of transcendental wonder. The minute brush strokes are distant echoes of Cézanne's *Petit Sensation*. They climb the structure of the bridge like triangular counterpoints to an engineer's soaring theme.

The Victorian cottage and the untidy warehouses in the foreground vainly struggle for notice, but they are overwhelmed by the intricacies of the bridge's structure and by its massive majesty. The lighting at the top of the picture, where the two steel arms will ultimately join, has a halo-like effect such as one might expect of a painting of the rising towers of Chartres Cathedral. Grace Cossington Smith's painting is indeed a Te Deum to progress.

The Bridge In-Curve

Sydney Harbour 1936
Oil on canvas. 91.5 × 122.5 cm
Art Gallery of New South Wales

John D. Moore *(1888–1958)*

John Drummond Moore was born at Waverley, Sydney, in 1888. He was a practising architect but all through his life he sketched and painted as well. He worked as an architect in New York for several years before the First World War and for a short time after the war. He spent the war years in the Royal Engineers serving in France. After the Armistice he began studying drawing at the Polytechnic Institute and architecture at the Architectural Association's School in London, achieving the distinction of becoming an Associate of the Royal Institute of British Architects. On his return to Australia he went into practice as an architect and lectured part-time at the University of Sydney. He continually painted and sketched and in 1925 had his first real exhibition in Sydney.

In 1933 Basil Burdett wrote in *Art in Australia:* 'John Moore was one of the painters who saw that all sunshine was making the Australian painter a very dull boy . . .' Moore's style was indeed a strong reaction against the sunny 'blue and gold' tradition of Streeton and Roberts; he was one of a number of artists who had become dissatisfied with the endless aping of the masters of the Heidelberg School. Moore wrote: 'Styles and isms are not important. They do not matter, if sometimes they happen to fit, use them. But don't let them use you.'

Again, in the words of Burdett: 'Strong skies, with tumbling clouds reflected in leaden seas and on darkened headlands and hills, marked his visual preferences. They more than hinted a weariness with perpetual sunshine and the unchanging mood which was thought to be proper to the typical Australian landscape.'

Moore's contribution to the expanding vision of the harbour is in a similar vein to Margaret Preston's and presents a dominant image of twentieth-century mechanization. In it the harbour is seen from a balcony of flats on the south side of the bridge.

There are few dancing lights on the water and little bustling activity. Moore shows the viewer a dullish day with wintry clouds overhanging the leaden waters of the harbour and city. There is a classical sense of stillness which is reinforced by the strong composition of the vertical and horizontal elements in the foreground. A frozenly placed still life of a towel, shell and plate, combined with the rigid steel rail, clearly indicate that Moore is interested in formalizing and intellectualizing an essentially romantic subject.

Sydney Harbour

Morning Haze

Morning Haze
Oil. 44 × 36 cm
Hinton Collection. Armidale College of Advanced Education and the Council of the City of Armidale

Robert Johnson *(1890–1964)*

Robert Johnson, born in Auckland, New Zealand, in 1890, studied at the Elam School of Art from 1910 to 1914 under Archibald Nicoll and Edward Fristrom. Fristrom, a Swedish painter, was, during his time, much praised for his use of colour.

When the war began, Johnson left art school and signed up as an artilleryman. After the war, he and two other veterans held exhibitions of war paintings around the main centres in New Zealand. A large work, *The Cloth Hall, Ypres*, was acquired by the Auckland National Gallery.

Several years later, in 1920, Johnson decided to come to Australia. He was immediately fascinated by Sydney—the harbour, the hills, the surrounding countryside. However, despite the visual spell which the city cast on the thirty-year-old New Zealander, Johnson appears to have had trouble settling into his new home. His first exhibition was presented seven years after he arrived at the Grosvenor Gallery, Sydney.

The exhibition caused a 'sensation' according to Walter Taylor, who wrote 'an appreciation' of his work in *Art in Australia* (February 1934). Sensation seems a somewhat strong word for a painter whose work, for the most part could easily be seen to be part of the Streeton Impressionist manner. However, what undoubtedly is true, is that Johnson became, over the years, a very popular painter in the drawing rooms around Sydney. Much sought-after were his many Harbour scenes, in which light and atmosphere were his trade marks.

As a painter, Johnson worked 'impressionistically' out in the open, often camping at the spot he had chosen to paint. Middle Harbour was one of his favourite subjects.

In *Morning Haze*, Johnson captures a familiar Sydney Harbour sight—the peek-a-boo glimpse of the water from the terrace houses of an inner suburb. While one cannot place the actual scene in this picture, the viewer has seen many like it from various vantage points around the Harbour.

The first thing one notices about the work is the pale blue light which suffuses the whole dappled and serene scene. The street, partly deserted, is framed by a tree on each side while down the road, at the bottom of the hill lies the harbour—itself quiet and caught in that blue mist of early morning light.

Sydney Harbour View 1907
Oil. 38 × 30.5 cm
Hinton Collection. Armidale College of Advanced Education and the Council of the City of Armidale.

Sydney Long *(1871–1955)*

Sydney Long was born in Goulburn, New South Wales, in 1871. He studied with Julian Ashton and A. J. Daplyn in Sydney, and then with Malcolm Osborne in London. He achieved some fame in London with his etchings and was elected an Associate of the Royal Society of Painters-Etchers. On his return to Australia he founded an Australian branch of this society and became its president.

'Sid' Long was Australia's most significant Art Nouveau artist. 'Art Nouveau,' writes Bernard Smith, 'suggested new ways of depicting Australian tree-forms. The thin graceful stems and feathery branches of eucalypt saplings and the sinuous lines of the tea-tree lent themselves splendidly to a decorative treatment.' Long played on the freedoms of the Art Nouveau style to create an enchanted new image of the Australian landscape. A dominant theme of Long's work was the man-beast Pan, the patron god of the 'naughty nineties'. By populating the Australian bush with the antics of this freedom-loving spirit, Long was, for the first time, introducing characters from classical mythology into Australian art.

The significance of Long's vision lay in the fact that the bush could be seen, at least metaphorically, as more than a threatening economic and agricultural encumbrance; it could now be looked upon as a place of liberation and freedom.

It was difficult to sustain this myth; the landscape was much too prickly, too straggly and uncomfortable to accommodate such a light-hearted and frivolous creature as the god Pan. In spite of this, Long managed to create pictures of enormous elegance and untroubled passion.

The public, however, was to some extent lukewarm. In the face of this response, writes Donald Friend, Long was too timid to let himself go and finally became 'a soured romantic'. For economic reasons, he was reduced to painting works which were mediocre and often banal.

Sydney Harbour View is both ornamental and decorative. There is a lack of delineation in the middle ground which gives a deliberate flatness, while the spindly trees on the right form a lacy frame for a vista which is characterized by placid emptiness and evocative abstraction. The painting has a sense of timelessness and suggests secrecy and a desire to escape from the realities of a pressing and threatening urbanization. Indeed, Sydney Long's vision of the harbour is one of timeless escapism.

Sydney Harbour View

Mosman Bay

Margaret Preston *(1875–1963)*

Mosman Bay c 1926
Handcoloured woodcut on mulberry paper. 25.4 × 18.5 cm
Australian National Gallery, Canberra

Sydney Heads c 1925
Handcoloured woodcut. 24.9 × 18.6 cm
Gift of Mrs Alison Brown
Art Gallery of New South Wales

Shell Cove Sydney c 1928
Hand tinted woodcut on thin Japanese paper. 21.6 × 27.1 cm
Australian National Gallery, Canberra

Born in Adelaide in 1875, Margaret Preston was the most popular woman artist of the twenties. She studied at the School of Design, Adelaide and at Melbourne's National Gallery School under Bernard Hall. After spending eight years studying and travelling in Europe, she returned to Australia in 1920 and very soon became a dominant figure in Australian post-Impressionism.

While in Europe Preston had been attracted to the principles of Fauvism, but she later rejected any suggestion of colour which was decoratively bright or too obviously light-hearted. By the mid-twenties her palette had become sombre with greys and blacks which were applied to strong geometric compositions with a Cézanne-like tendency to structural emphasis.

In her treatment of the flora and fauna of Australia, Preston was able to make a leap of the imagination which combined Cubist principles with an intuitive sense of design. One aspect of her genius is that she never lapsed into mere decoration.

Margaret Preston's constant exhortation to Australian artists was to look at their own country rather than to imitate European styles. Her word of advice was: 'search for the root'. In Sydney Ure Smith's publication *Margaret Preston's Monotypes*, Margaret Preston wrote of this search for cultural identity: 'We are a nation of people who are growing up and who should not acquire a counterfeit culture by borrowing the intellect of all countries'. She recognized the beauty of Aboriginal art and closely studied rock cave and bark paintings. She recommended that the serious painter study these, not as a 'model', 'but as an aesthetic form which is of our land'. The idea of some of her monotypes, she wrote, was to 'show the potentialities of an art that has intellectual differences from that of other countries', always recognizing, however, that 'every artist must work from his own temperament'.

Preston's woodcuts of Sydney Harbour are notable for their compressed starkness. The forms are arranged as if she were designing them for stained glass windows. She was not interested in the atmospheric effects, the grand spatial vistas, or the hedonistic qualities which had inspired others.

Her vision of the harbour is in one sense limited by the treatment of the bay as an elaborate arrangement of geometric forms. At the same time, the manner in which she states her case is daring and is in keeping with the spirit of her time.

Sydney Heads

Shell Cove Sydney

Sydney Harbour

John Peter Russell *(1859–1930)*

Sydney Harbour
Watercolour. 47.8 × 61.2 cm
Australian National Gallery,
Canberra

John Peter Russell was one of Australia's finest exponents of French Impressionism. He was born in Sydney and very early acquired a passion for art and for the sea. After inheriting a private income upon the death of his father, he went to England to study at the Slade School in London. From London he went to Paris where he met, and was greatly influenced by, Rodin, Van Gogh, Monet and others. He married Rodin's favourite model, Marianna Antionetta Matiocco, and they made their home at Belle Ile off the coast of Brittany, raising seven children in idyllic surroundings. Here Russell painted his most sunny and lyrical paintings.

When his wife died in 1908, Russell settled his children in European boarding schools and left Belle Ile. He remarried in 1912 and spent the years of the First World War in England. After the war, with a fresh burst of energy and inspiration, he renewed his painting activities in Switzerland, France and Italy. He had now been away from Australia for forty years.

In 1923 Russell and his wife returned to Australia to make their home in Sydney. But for Russell the homecoming was a disappointment. He was unrecognized and little interest was shown in his work. His offer of a collection of modern French art was rejected by the official art world of Sydney, and the priceless collection remained in France. It is from this period of disappointment that the present watercolour of Rose Bay emerged.

Despite the artist's obvious depression, the painting, *Sydney Harbour*, has a breezy, light-hearted atmosphere. The scene, the harbour filled with racing sailing boats, would have appealed to Russell's sportsman's heart as well as to his artistic sensibilities. In a few lightning brushstrokes and washes, Russell has captured the airy salty sense of wind-filled sails and glistening water against the framework of a leafy suburban hill.

Potts Point 1957
Oil on canvas. 51 × 71 cm
Collection: James Fairfax

Sali Herman *(b. 1898)*

Sali Herman was born in Zurich in 1898. He studied in Zurich and Paris and then spent some years as an art dealer, travelling extensively in Europe, the Americas and Africa. He arrived in Australia in 1937 and studied at the George Bell School in Melbourne.

Herman is known particularly for his paintings of the façade of old houses and for their unique surface texture. 'Houses to me', he said, 'are a part of life as it is, just as human beings are. An old man or an old woman may not be attractive but may have beauty in their character. So it is with houses. When I paint them I look for the character of prettiness or dirty walls.'

After his studies in Melbourne, Herman moved to Potts Point, Sydney. Potts Point, with its inner city atmosphere and cheap rooms for rent, was a natural habitat for the avant-garde artists of the day. As Laurie Thomas notes: 'In those days the whole of that area was alive with artists, all utterly different yet full of conviction and rubbing sparks off each other—Olsen, Drysdale, Herman, Rapotec, Meadmore, Upward, Hessing, Hughes, Klippel, Rose, Passmore—most of them actually living there.' The Kings Cross–Potts Point area had become Sydney's waterfront Montmartre. Its artists, high above the city and protected by slender Victorian iron balustrades, could watch the huge cargo ships berthed beside the docks flanked with long warehouses, and see in the distance the skyline of the city.

Potts Point, which won the 1944 Wynne prize, is typical of Herman's work. It is a happy treatment of the McElhone Stairs which joined Woolloomooloo to Potts Point. The strong horizontal formed by the fence appears to stabilize the crooked, crumbling, cubed shapes of the terraces. The chimneys punctuate the blue of the sky and act as decorative elements. Herman has added human interest by including a man staring out of a window, an old woman feeding cats and a child sitting in the gutter.

It is interesting to note that the house on the corner is now an elegant art gallery specializing in colonial Australian paintings.

Potts Point

Vanished View 1948
Oil on canvas. 58.5 × 78.5 cm
Collection: Shay Docking

Desiderius Orban *(b. 1884)*

Desiderius Orban was born in Hungary in 1884. In Budapest he established an art school and when he arrived in Sydney in 1939 he did the same. Orban was a stimulating teacher and an inspiration to students for many years. The beginning of the nineteen-forties saw the arrival of a large number of Europeans to the Sydney art scene. Many, like Desiderius Orban, came as a result of Hitler's threat to Europe, but few had as profound an effect on Australian art as did this talented Hungarian.

Orban was self-taught, except for a brief two weeks at the *Académie Julian* in Paris, but he spent his formative years travelling between Budapest and Paris. In Paris he was a frequent guest of Gertrude Stein's famous Saturday afternoon 'at homes' where he met Picasso, Modigliani and Matisse. When the Academy of Modern Arts and Crafts was founded in Budapest in 1933, Orban became its director. In 1938 he resigned to emigrate to Australia.

After the Second World War, in which he served in the Australian Army, Orban set up a studio at Circular Quay which, after a shaky beginning, began to attract some of the most talented young artists of the city. These included Judy Cassab, Margo Lewers and John Olsen. Orban, a dedicated teacher, instructed his students in the techniques of oils, charcoal and watercolour. But he did more than that; he imparted to them his fervent belief in the difference between a painter and an artist. A painter, he said, was someone who had learned the trade of pictures, but an artist was one who could 'put the world before the spectator'. 'Every work of art,' he wrote, 'emanates a kind of spirituality . . . the full responsibility of creativeness is rejecting the help of outside influence.'

Orban's *Vanished View* (1948), painted near the site of his studio at the Rocks, shows the Harbour Bridge, George Street, the Quay crowded with boats, and the picturesque towers and dilapidated buildings of the old city. The artist has masterfully organized all these complex forms into two dynamic curves—the road and the bridge—which complement each other, while the bows of the boats create minor motifs. The striking verticals of the telegraph poles are echoed in the stanchions of the bridge and in the funnels and factory towers.

Orban, unlike many other artists, sees the harbour as intimately connected with the city, inseparable from it and pushing deeply into its arteries. Ferries and barges tied to the dock are almost indistinguishable from the houses. The scene is sombre and touched with a romantic European melancholy. Evidently Orban prefers the harbour when the winter sun is overcast, the light generally grey and the mood reflective.

Vanished View

Boy and Sea Bird 1951
Oil on hardboard. 86.5 × 175.5 cm
Australian National Gallery,
Canberra

John Passmore *(b. 1904)*

John Passmore, born in Sydney in 1904, spent his boyhood playing around the boatsheds of Lavender Bay in Sydney. After leaving school in 1917 at the age of thirteen he spent his time with his father, who worked on the boats. 'The German sea captains, the smell of the bilges being pumped out, the feel of the ropes, the noise of the men are still as real to me now as then,' he said in a rare interview in 1976, 'I belonged to the children of the street—except at tea time.'

Passmore studied under Julian Ashton and George Lambert at the Sydney Art School between 1918 and 1933. He remarked 'I was born in the Edwardian Age. Julian Ashton was my teacher. All the men went at night and the women during the day. The real artists went at night time.' In 1933 he went to England where he remained for seventeen years. He returned to Australia with an intense interest in Picasso, Cézanne and abstract construction.

In Sydney again, Passmore taught at the Julian Ashton School and East Sydney Technical College. He had a strong influence on students such as John Olsen, William Rose and Peter Upward. Passmore's patrician, demanding and disciplined nature made him one of the seminal figures in Sydney painting in the fifties. In 1959 he went back to Europe for a year and on his return he stopped exhibiting his works and went into seclusion. He said 'I gave up exhibiting because when you are working at something it is you—you are the paintings. Everyone has a secret. My studio and my paintings are my secret, myself.'

For eighteen years very few people have seen Passmore. He shows his work to no one. 'I have in my flat spider webs that have been being spun for ten years,' he said, 'I like dust and darkness. The other day I went to the Christie Auction rooms to see one of the pictures, but I really went to see all those paintings that belong to the period of love—to see Conder, Long, Roberts, Gruner—in those days there wasn't any money around, and artists just painted for love.'

Passmore's harbour is an arena for human drama—for tragedy, the bizarre and the quixotic. The artist and his painting have been engulfed by the Age of Anxiety, and the stiff and clumsy figures express some internal sense of doom and disaster. In *Boy and Sea Bird* there is little joy or spectacular sexuality. Passmore's swimmers are anxiety-ridden, shrouded in sinister grey and threatening oily greens. A seagull is pecking at one of the figures, while other swimmers watch in a mood that is more predatory than that of the bird. The setting for this painting is an enclosed Victorian bathing area, the old Domain Baths located at Woolloomooloo, Sydney Harbour.

Boy and Sea Bird

Sydney Harbour 1978
Oil and enamel. 92 × 122 cm
Collection of the artist

Sidney Nolan *(b. 1917)*

Sidney Nolan was born in Melbourne in 1917. He attended various art schools in Melbourne including the National Gallery School. The president of the Contemporary Art Society, John Reed, became interested in his pictures and subsequently became his patron. Sir Kenneth Clark, who came to Australia in 1947, was also fascinated by Nolan's work and called him 'Australia's only real painter'. He later had a showing of paintings in Paris and a large retrospective exhibition in the Whitechapel Gallery, London, in 1957. Of all Australian artists, Sidney Nolan has the greatest reputation overseas.

Nolan has been continually inspired by myth, literature and heroic stories of adventure, many of which have an underlying theme of freedom. He has depicted, for example, Leda and the Swan, the shipwreck of Mrs Fraser, the Eureka Stockade, the explorers Burke and Wills and has executed a series of paintings based on the Gallipoli campaign.

By temperament Nolan is a restless traveller, constantly visiting and revisiting China, Africa, Antarctica and Australia. Nolan's view of Sydney Harbour, painted 20 April 1978, is the vision of a traveller. As John Russell, then critic for the *London Times*, wrote in *Art and Australia* (September 1967), 'Nolan is at home everywhere, in all countries and all societies.'

It is rare for Nolan to paint cities. He is more at home painting deserts, the animals of the savannah country in Africa, the Antarctic, or the timbered country of Ned Kelly. This painting is one of the few Nolan has done of Sydney Harbour. However, in England in 1977, he did some sea-paintings inspired by Benjamin Britten's operas, *Billy Budd* and *Peter Grimes*.

Nolan's *Sydney Harbour* takes a relaxed, tourist's view. It was, in fact, painted from a suite in one of Sydney's de luxe hotels. It is interesting to remember that Matisse and Bonnard often painted in hotels in France. Executed from a high vantage point, the painting has a spontaneous freshness, an unexpected brevity and a compositional directness that is often a hallmark of Nolan's style. Noticeable is the manner in which the artist reduces the foreshores to a strong figure-eight shape, minimizes the activity on the harbour, and lets the broad expanse of water dominate the buildings. The city appears transient and ephemeral against the land and the water.

As Nolan presents the scene, it has an earthy dryness that is reminiscent of Tripoli, Alexandria or the outback. He avoids any sensuous atmospheric effects, decorative detailing or play of light on the surfaces. Despite the clustering of modern buildings in the foreground, Nolan's *Sydney Harbour* evokes an ancient image. Even the Opera House, a central image in the picture, has been transformed into an exotic pyramid, which might well exist on the shores of an imagined inland sea, salty and remote.

Sydney Harbour

Sydney Harbour No. 2 1978
Oil on canvas. 121 × 152 cm
Collection of the artist

Arthur Boyd *(b. 1920)*

Arthur Boyd was born in Murrumbeena, Victoria, in 1920. His father, Merric Boyd, was a naive potter and painter. He influenced his son deeply in the experience of the Old and New Testaments and these have been a constant theme in Boyd's work. Boyd had very little formal training and spent many of his early years painting in the bush with his grandfather and friends.

After the Second World War, which had a most disturbing effect on him, Boyd's painting became more expressionistic. His contact with Percival, Tucker and the Russian emigre Danila Vassilieff deepened his belief in mythology and symbolism as the basis of his work.

In 1960 Boyd went to London where he enhanced his already considerable reputation. He now lives in Nowra and London.

After returning from London in 1978 Boyd, on a June afternoon, took a sentimental ferry ride to Mosman and Sirius Cove, the site of the artists' camps in the late nineteenth and early twentieth centuries. Enthralled, Boyd remained on the ferry, making notes and sketches until it became dark.

'I went on the ferry', he remarked, 'to experience the shapes the forms and the light. After living in places like Suffolk and Italy where the light is pale and impressionistic it is always a surprise, despite the mental image you have of Australia, to see that the light is so light, and the dark is so dark.'

Boyd, the magician of psychological tension, has in his *Sydney Harbour No. 2* created a mood of sombre winter quietude. It is a view often seen by ferry commuters coming from Circular Quay.

Except for the houses, whose small lights peer out at us like eyes in a forest, Boyd's harbour is wild, rocky, dark and untamed. The water is untrammelled by man, bird, boats or any remnants of civilized activity. The bush foreshore hangs over us, gnarled and weather-beaten, foreboding, mysterious and melancholy. It is Boyd's elegy to the harbour.

'To me', Boyd said of this, his first harbour painting, 'the little lights in the houses were forlorn attempts to civilize the place. The houses looked as if they were clinging on. It doesn't have the well-established look of a European water city. The lights looked like feeble attempts to come to grips with a wilderness.'

Sydney Harbour No. 2

Five Bells No. 1

Five Bells No. 1
Oil on hardboard. 264.5 × 274 cm
Collection: G. Clarke

Entrance to the Seaport of Desire 1964
Acrylic on canvas. 167.6 × 213.4 cm
Gift of Mrs M. S. McGrath
Art Gallery of New South Wales

The Ship Passes By 1973
Oil on wood panel. 183 × 244 cm
Collection: Mrs A Purves

John Olsen *(b. 1928)*

Among all the painters who have been challenged or captivated by the harbour, it is, perhaps, in the work of John Olsen that we find the most complex, multidimensional, mysterious and provocative of images.

From the mid-sixties to the early seventies, Olsen found in the thriving scenes of harbour life a rich, bristling energy. The harbour, encrusted with cranes and docks and sprinkled with sails, its foreshores teeming with brightly coloured lines of traffic and its waters raucously alive with animal and plant life, was, for Olsen, a miraculously textured visual feast. Using an energetic, abstract expressionistic technique interspersed with figurative elements, he created canvas after canvas of works celebrating the topographical wonder of the harbour.

Entrance to the Seaport of Desire is certainly the master painting from this period. It has a baroque lushness and exuberance, and a complexity which has been magnificently sustained. As the title of the painting reveals, Olsen is viewing the harbour as a significant symbol of man's state of sin. Thus we see its inlets and coves and vast expanse of water crowded almost into insignificance by the chaos along its foreshores, brilliantly suggested by the intertwining lines and forms.

John Olsen writes in his book *Salute to Five Bells*, 'this picture is about Sydney Harbour on a hot January day—the mad rat race tempo of Sydney's traffic—the waxy fluid, juicy fruit tempo, that vibrant vulgarity—"Ello John 'ows the misses awright?"

'I've always thought that the formation of Sydney's land forms like a bitch goddess and frankly at times it frightens me. The breasty contours of its hills and when your (*sic*) sailing through the heads you feel as though your (*sic*) sailing through her arms—and when you are coming into to (*sic*) her you feel you are going deeper and you are caught in her spidery net.'

In 1970, Olsen was asked by the Dobell Foundation to execute a huge mural for the newly completed Sydney Opera House. He chose for the theme Kenneth Slessor's poem *Five Bells*, whose lyrical invocations of the sea, anecdotal qualities and descriptions of the harbour provided a perfect literary springboard, even though its theme was the drowning of a man.

A vast physical and stylistic distance separates the two paintings. The mural could well have been in the violent and chaotic mood of the early work. Instead, Olsen puts the viewer under the sea and magically produces a hushed calm, radiant with luminescent forms which unite the surface. The most interesting qualities of the mural are its stunning simplicity and its beautiful use of space.

With these, and with other works, Olsen has transformed the harbour into a contemporary image in which the viewer may find a lyrical majesty or a disturbing message.

Entrance to the Seaport of Desire

The Ship Passes By

Beare's Park, Elizabeth Bay 1961
Oil on canvas. 64 × 78 cm
Collection: Bank of New South Wales

Jeffrey Smart *(b. 1921)*

Jeffrey Smart, born in Adelaide in 1921, studied at the School of Arts and Crafts in Adelaide and later in France. He worked as a teacher, as art critic for the Sydney *Daily Telegraph* and as compere of a children's art programme for the Australian Broadcasting Commission. Today he lives in Italy.

Smart, it could be said, stands as a bridge between the two generations of figurative artists. His man-made environments, peopled by humans that are isolated, dwarfed or perplexed by their surroundings, belong to the world of Hopper, while his loaded time sense catches some of the distilled moments of Weyth. At the same time, Smart's link with the younger artists can be seen in his enthusiasm for the modern shapes and forms of contemporary life—airports, throughways, office buildings, billboards, buses, trucks and traffic signs.

Smart's organization of a picture plane is, in concept, close to Cézanne's 'cube, cone, cylinder' theory. He often uses space as a 'box' in which figures and architectural elements are carefully balanced in almost classical mathematical relationships. The subject matter, he says, 'is only the hinge that opens the door, the hook on which one hangs the coat. My only concern is putting the right shapes in the right colours in the right places. It is always the geometry.'

In *Beare's Park, Elizabeth Bay*, painted while Smart was art critic for the *Daily Telegraph*, there is a sharp contrast between the orderliness of a small, crisp Victorian park and the turbulence of the harbour. The latter, dramatized by stark geometric composition in dark forbidding colours, is a scene of disquiet and imminent danger. A freak wind has created a spiralling whirlpool. There is a generating power present, invisible and incomprehensible, but it is a godless power. Smart seeks to create a psychological dread in the viewer by emphasizing the emptiness of the park and the foreboding nature of the sea.

Beare's Park, Elizabeth Bay

Sydney Harbour 1973
Gouache on paper. 31 × 73 cm
Collection: Rudy Komon

Fred Williams *(b. 1927)*

Fred Williams, known primarily as a landscape painter, is not a Sydney-sider, however, like Sidney Nolan, Tom Roberts, Arthur Streeton, and Arthur Boyd, four other eminent Victorians, he has, on occasion, been inspired to paint Sydney Harbour.

While Sydney is unfamiliar terrain for Williams, his strip images subtly reveal the aspects of the harbour city which most capture his imagination. Williams is not interested in painting the harbour as an arena of bustling commercial activity, or as a yachtsman's paradise —nor does he find it an interesting visual metaphor—what Williams does find challenging is the light, as well as the space.

In some aspects, Williams' painting is close to Sidney Nolan's *Sydney Harbour*. Both take a panoramic view of Sydney and the harbour, and in both artists' works there is the feeling of the traveller, the passer-by.

The appeal for Williams, as seen in this work, *Sydney Harbour*, aside from the sheer scale of the harbour, is the quality of light which has tantalised past and present painters. Sydney light is unique. The high pitched, clear blue sky is an atmospheric window of this city. To capture this curious light condition, Williams has used a cameraman's device. He spans the harbour in a slow arc, letting the sky fill the 'lens', to the point of distancing the cityscape into an insignificant landmass.

Frederick Williams was born in Melbourne in 1927. He was, on his own admission, 'a flat-footed student' who went to school part time or full-time for years. Williams disciplined himself sufficiently to study painting for two or three years with George Bell, before going to England to the Chelsea Art School. There he did six years. 'By any standards,' he once said, 'I was a very dogged sort of pupil. I wasn't in a hurry.'

When Williams arrived back in Australia he was struck by how 'odd' the landscape appeared: 'It always worried me that there was no focal point in the landscape here,' he told John Monks in an interview, 'so I simply thought well I'll paint it and I'll leave the focal point out. And, of course, the epitome of that is my strip paintings. I just let them read as they are.'

In essence this is exactly the same principle which Williams has used in his view of Sydney Harbour. He simply allows the harbour and city to be 'read'. He doesn't single out a place, an image, a landmark or a building to attract the attention of the viewer.

Sydney Harbour

Harbour
Six watercolours. 180 × 255 cm
Collection of the artist

Charles Blackman *(b. 1928)*

Charles Blackman's work is essentially an expression of his own emotional experiences as they relate to the people, places and things around him. His paintings have a gentleness, sensitivity and colour that has been compared with the poetry of Shaw Neilson.

Charles Blackman was born in Sydney in 1928, but spent his early years in Queensland. He studied art at the East Sydney Technical College and worked for five years as an artist for the Sydney *Sun* before going to Melbourne. In Melbourne, Blackman helped with the re-formation of the Contemporary Art Society and emerged as a promising artist in his exhibitions at the Gallery of Contemporary Art.

In 1960 he went to England where he achieved considerable success. His work was included in the Whitechapel and Tate Gallery exhibitions of Australian art (1961 and 1962–3).

After his return from overseas, Blackman chose Sydney as his home. He explains his choice in these words:

> As a visual being I love the splendour of Sydney Harbour—although I feel that Paris is the most fit city for a painter to live in, and although the south Queensland light, shimmering between green mountains and blue seas at Surfers Paradise, suits me best as a painter. I do not choose to live in a harbourside house. I like the surprises of the harbour seen from a balcony, glimpsed between tall buildings, at the turn of a road, in the solace of evening or on the bleakest winter mornings.
>
> Had I been brought up tied to the apron strings of Old Mother Harbour, I should probably have seen her from the midst of her waters as a sailing man. But instead, in this city of waters, I grew up at Freshwater, riding the breakers, diving from cliffs, watching the shark patrols and surf carnivals. So this is what I go on painting—swimmers and beach people, and only occasionally the harbour.

In this series of watercolours Blackman has attempted to catch the harbour's multiplicity of moods and scenic changes—from the red-roofed houses of South Head dominated by the towering rocky cliffs, to the calm sandy beaches and coves of Watson's Bay and Elizabeth Bay.

Blackman's view of the harbour is essentially hedonistic. The harbour is a scenic playground in which the senses can be indulged. It is interesting to note that there are only a few pictures in existence of people actually bathing in the harbour. When one compares the two swimming figures in the lower left panel of Blackman's *Harbour* with the nightmarish painting by John Passmore, *Boy and Sea Bird*, one can instantly see that Blackman's intentions are quite different. Blackman's mood is relaxed and casual; Passmore's is anguished and electrically intense.

Harbour

Big Kite

John Firth-Smith *(b. 1943)*

Big Kite
Oil on canvas. 90 × 130 cm
Private collection

Bombora and Boats
Oil on canvas. 116 × 106 cm
Collection: J. D. Kahlbetzer

South Head and Pipe Smoke
Oil on canvas. 122 × 152.5 cm
Private collection

John Firth-Smith was born in Melbourne in 1943 and studied at the Julian Ashton School in Sydney as well as the East Sydney Technical College.

His early works, such as *Big Kite*, feature Sydney Harbour as a yachtsman's paradise, with sailing boats tracing elegant arcs as they skim through blue waters, their spinnakers filling space with striped Byzantine splendour.

In his more recent works this presentation of the harbour as a playground for sportsmen has given way to a harbour dominated by huge container ships. Firth-Smith uses the waterlines, form and colour schemes of the ships to create handsome, compelling abstract works.

While Firth-Smith is unsure of his antecedents, he claims an affinity with Aboriginal art, Ian Fairweather and an appreciation of the enthusiasm and freedom of John Olsen. He maintains that his art happens without a premeditated or intellectual premise.

Two elements contribute to Firth-Smith's art: firstly, a belief in the art of craftsmanship as manifested in boat-building, and, secondly, the belief that art is concerned with 'happenings', with processes of nature. His eye is that of a mason while his talents are directed to a more esoteric rendering of fact and visual experience.

Firth-Smith's involvement with boats and the world of the sea goes back to his childhood . . . 'Since I was a little kid I always made things—yachts, for example, which I sent off to sea with little notes on the deck so that if they ever got to South America they might write back.'

If there is a puzzle for this artist it is the fact that art does not *do* anything—the way boats do.

The three pictures represented belong to an earlier period—when Firth-Smith used the harbour as a flat arena in which to explore space. In *South Head and Pipe Smoke*, for example, a speedboat breaks the flatness of the blue surface in a flurry of circular agitated movement. This is made even more dramatic by Firth-Smith's introduction of three pincer-like land masses, rendered in strips of black, red and green. The speedboat cracks the water between the landmarks as a bullet might flash through the air.

Certainly no other artist has ever rendered the harbour's playground duality more dynamically, in contemporary terms, than Firth-Smith.

In essence this is exactly the same principle which Williams has used in his view of Sydney Harbour. He simply allows the harbour and city to be 'read'. He doesn't single out a place, an image, a landmark or a building to attract the attention of the viewer.

Bombora and Boats

South Head and Pipe Smoke

Big Orange (Sunset)

Brett Whiteley *(b. 1939)*

Big Orange (Sunset) 1974
Acrylic on canvas. 244 × 305 cm
Gift of Patrick White
Art Gallery of New South Wales

The Jacaranda Tree (On Sydney Harbour) 1977
Oil on canvas. 208 × 456 cm
Private collection

Lavender Bay in the Rain 1974
Oil on plywood. 101.6 × 76.2 cm
Collection: M. B. and L. C. Hilliard

Among contemporary painters Brett Whiteley has established himself as the unquestioned master of Sydney Harbour—or at least a portion of it, Lavender Bay.

In 1970, after some years in London and two years in New York, Whiteley arrived back in Australia. He and his wife, Wendy, bought a three-storey wood and brick house at Lavender Bay, a hilly urban watery retreat on the northern shore of the city.

Architecturally the house was without character, but its surroundings—an overgrown park to the left, dominated by a large Moreton Bay fig, and the superb bay in front—more than compensated for its architectural weaknesses.

Having set up a studio, Whiteley began to explore, in paint and pen, the seemingly endless variety of scenes which flooded each window of the house.

The views were both dramatic and intimate: looking down the hill was the Lavender Bay ferry wharf, around which nestled small sailboats and cruisers; rising theatrically behind this was the Harbour Bridge from under which the 'sails' of the Opera House peeked; and spreading westward were green foreshores with an occasional boatyard.

Magnificent palms, purple-blossomed jacarandas and flame trees surrounded the area. A steep rickety set of steps leading from the house to the wharf gave an additional Montmartre atmosphere to the setting.

To enrich this already exotic environment there was yet another unusual visual factor that bewitched Whiteley's view. A pink and green turreted amusement park, Luna Park, complete with gigantic smiling face, glittering roller coasters, whirlygigs and tuneful merry-go-round, dominated the scene to the left of his house.

As if all this was not enough, there was still the bay itself, an enchanted waterway of moving craft, shifting moods and changing lights. For Whiteley, after two harsh and disappointing years in New York, the scene was paradise. In rain (as portrayed in *Lavender Bay in the Rain*) or bright sunlight, in the evening and at dawn, Whiteley put down his impressions. Some of the works were descriptive, even analytical in detail; others such as *Big Orange* were almost completely abstract.

At times he rendered the waters of the bay in a Whistlerian grey, at others in a buttery wheat colour or a bright lipstick orange. More often than not, however, he chose his favourite colour—the brilliant and lush ultramarine blue that is seen in *The Jacaranda Tree (On Sydney Harbour)*.

Stylistically Whiteley used a technique he had perfected in England with his well-known Christie series and London Zoo series. He described this style as a matter of 'focus'.

'Focus' for Whiteley meant deciding which objects, lines or forms he wanted to articulate clearly (often in minute detail) and which he wanted to blur, smudge or smear.

The Jacaranda Tree (On Sydney Harbour)

Lavender Bay in the Rain

Woolloomooloo Bay 1964
Oil on hardboard. 122 × 122 cm
Art Gallery of Western Australia

Kevin Connor *(b. 1932)*

For some inexplicable reason Sydney painters are rarely Expressionists. Kevin Connor is by far the most original and talented of the artists who work in this particular style.

Connor, a native of Sydney, was born in 1932 and trained at the East Sydney Technical College. The winner of many prizes including several Archibald prizes for portraiture, the Sir William Angliss Memorial Art Prize, as well as a Harkness fellowship for study and travel in 1966, Connor has always been a painter of Sydney and its environs. For over a dozen years the Haymarket district of the city occupied his interest. In the works from this period, Connor reflects a sombre and anguished mood. His figures, often melting facelessly into crowds, depict the anonymity of the urban dweller. In some of these early Expressionist works one can almost smell the sense of fear or despair that engulfs these figures. In more recent years Connor's mood appears to have lifted, without sacrificing the emotional intensity or energy which he wrestles from the paint.

In 1979 when Connor's *Poet and City* won the *Sydney Morning Herald* art award, he acknowledged that for thirty years the magic of Sydney had been an obsession with him. Certainly Connor's view of the harbour and city from Woolloomooloo is most unusual. Unlike Whiteley, Rees and Firth-Smith, Connor activates the scene with an almost frightening explosion of paint. His style, like his comment, is quite different from these other artists. The city, seen from an aerial perspective, appears to hold the dockside harbour between two gigantic pincers. Skyscrapers, cranes, freeways, warehouses, huge container ships and sleek white ocean liners have become entangled in a mesh of muddy reds, blacks, oranges and yellows. It is a lyrical web of fluid paint. Underlying Connor's vision of the city is the concept that it is a breathing organism whose symbiotic relationship with the harbour is at once violent and magnificent. Despite the fact that there are no human figures in the work, the human content is implied in *Woolloomooloo Bay*. Cities are man-made, and Connor seems torn between believing that what man has created is a glowering monster or a masterwork of poetry.

Woolloomooloo Bay

Procession and Cliffs

Shay Docking *(b. 1928)*

Procession and Cliffs 1977
Pastel on paper mounted on hardboard. 88 × 76 cm
Collection of the artist

Landfall 1975
Pastel on acrylic on paper on hardboard. 81 × 340 cm
Private collection

'Here is ancient Australia, at the very heads of Sydney Harbour. At South Head, great wind-sculptured boulders, sunbaked into warm orange reds, have no part in the busloads of tourists. North Head—sheer, vertical, proclaiming the land. Abrupt edge and immensity of ocean space flows into and through the heads, and the harbour within shelters, embraces the city.'

While these notes from Shay Docking's diary relate primarily to the painting, *The Entrance to the Harbour*, they nevertheless give general expression to her deep sympathy with the primordial forces of nature. Her earlier works are, in fact, dominated by such images as volcanoes, gorges and gnarled ancient geological formations—witnesses to an era unseen by human eyes.

Although many more famous names have preceded hers, Docking's vision of the harbour is unique in its own right and soberingly correct. Her works have a muscular and unromanticized character that is in the tradition of Margaret Preston—blunt, direct and uncompromising. Her harbour, despite spinnakers filled with easterly winds and hillsides dotted with red-roofed suburban dwellings, is a place of infinite age, patience and mysterious beginnings.

If the first colonial painters had been able to confront the alien landscape of the new colony without their prejudices and bitter memories of loss, their visions might well have approximated to those of Shay Docking.

Shay Docking studied at the Melbourne National Gallery School and at Swinburne Technical College. Her works have been included in travelling exhibitions of Australian art in South East Asia and the United States of America.

Landfall

Selected Bibliography

FREE, RENEE, *Lloyd Rees* (Lansdowne Australian Art Library, Melbourne, 1972)

GALBALLY, ANN, *Arthur Streeton* (Lansdowne Australian Art Library, Melbourne, 1971)

GALBALLY, ANN, *The Art of John Peter Russell* (Sun Books, Melbourne, 1977)

GLEESON, JAMES, *Colonial Painters 1788–1880* (Lansdowne Australian Art Library, Melbourne, 1971)

GLEESON JAMES, *Impressionist Painters 1881–1930* (Lansdowne Australian Art Library, Melbourne, 1971)

GLEESON, JAMES, *Modern Painters 1931–1970* (Lansdowne Australian Art Library, Melbourne, 1971)

HACKFORTH-JONES, JOCELYN, *Convict Artists* (Macmillan of Australia, Melbourne, 1977)

HOFF, URSULA, *Charles Conder* (Lansdowne Australian Art Library, Melbourne, 1972)

HUGHES, ROBERT, *The Art of Australia* (Penguin Books, Harmondsworth, Revised edition 1970)

LYNN, ELWYN, *The Australian Landscape and its Artists* (Bay Books, Sydney, 1977)

MEREDITH, MRS CHARLES, *Notes and sketches of New South Wales, during a residence in that Colony from 1839 to 1844* (Penguin Colonial Facsimiles, Ringwood, 1973. First published 1844)

MCCULLOCH, ALAN, *Encyclopedia of Australian Art* (Hutchinson of Australia, Melbourne, 1969)

MOUROT, SUZANNE, *This was Sydney: a pictorial history from 1788 to the present time* (Ure Smith, Sydney, 1969)

NEWLING, C. B., *A Memorial Volume to Howard Hinton, Patron of Art* (Angus & Robertson, Sydney, 1951)

OLSEN, JOHN, *Salute to Five Bells* (Angus & Robertson, Sydney, 1973)

PRINGLE, JOHN DOUGLAS, *Australian Painting Today* (Thames & Hudson, London, 1963)

REES, LLOYD, *The Small Treasures of a Lifetime* (Ure Smith, Sydney, 1969)

RIENITS, REX and THEA, *Early Artists of Australia* (Angus & Robertson, Sydney, 1963)

SMITH, BERNARD, *Australian Painting 1788–1960* (Oxford University Press, Melbourne, 1965)

SMITH, BERNARD, *Documents on art and taste in Australia* (Oxford University Press, Melbourne, 1975)

SMITH, BERNARD, *European Vision and the South Pacific 1768–1850* (Oxford University Press, London, 1960)

SMITH, BERNARD, *Place Taste and Tradition* (Ure Smith Sydney, 1945)

SPATE, VIRGINIA, *Tom Roberts* (Lansdowne Australian Art Library, Melbourne, 1972)

STEPHENSON, P. R., *The History and Description of Sydney Harbour* (Rigby, Adelaide, 1966)

URE SMITH, SYDNEY (ed.), *Margaret Preston's Monotypes* (Ure Smith, Sydney, no date)

Various issues of *Art in Australia* and *Art and Australia*

INDEX

Acknowledgements

The authors wish to thank painters, private collectors, galleries and public collections for their co-operation in allowing paintings to be photographed, or, in some cases, making available their own transparencies, and for granting permission to reproduce paintings. Paintings from State Galleries and Public Collections are reproduced by kind permission of the Trustees of the following: National Gallery, Canberra, the National Library of Australia, the Art Gallery of New South Wales, the Dixson Galleries, the Mitchell Library, the National Gallery of Victoria, the Ballarat Fine Art Gallery, and the Hinton Collection, College of Advanced Education and the Council of the City of Armidale. For assistance during the researching of material for this book, we wish to thank personally the following for their help: Mrs Brzostowski and Mrs Jessie Birch, National Gallery, Canberra; Miss Barbara Perry, and especially Mrs Sylvia Carr, National Library, Canberra; Ms Jacqueline Menzies, assistant curator of Australian Art, the curatorial staff and also Mr Sam Alcorn, Librarian, of the Art Gallery of New South Wales; the staff of the Mitchell and Dixson Libraries; and Ms Eileen Chanin, Director of the Macquarie Gallery, Sydney.

Also Douglas Thompson, photographer, who photographed the Sidney Nolan painting. Finally, the authors are indebted to John Olsen, Sydney painter, for generously giving his time, advice and support.

Thanks also to Mrs M. H. Streeton for generously granting permission to reproduce the paintings of Sir Arthur Streeton.

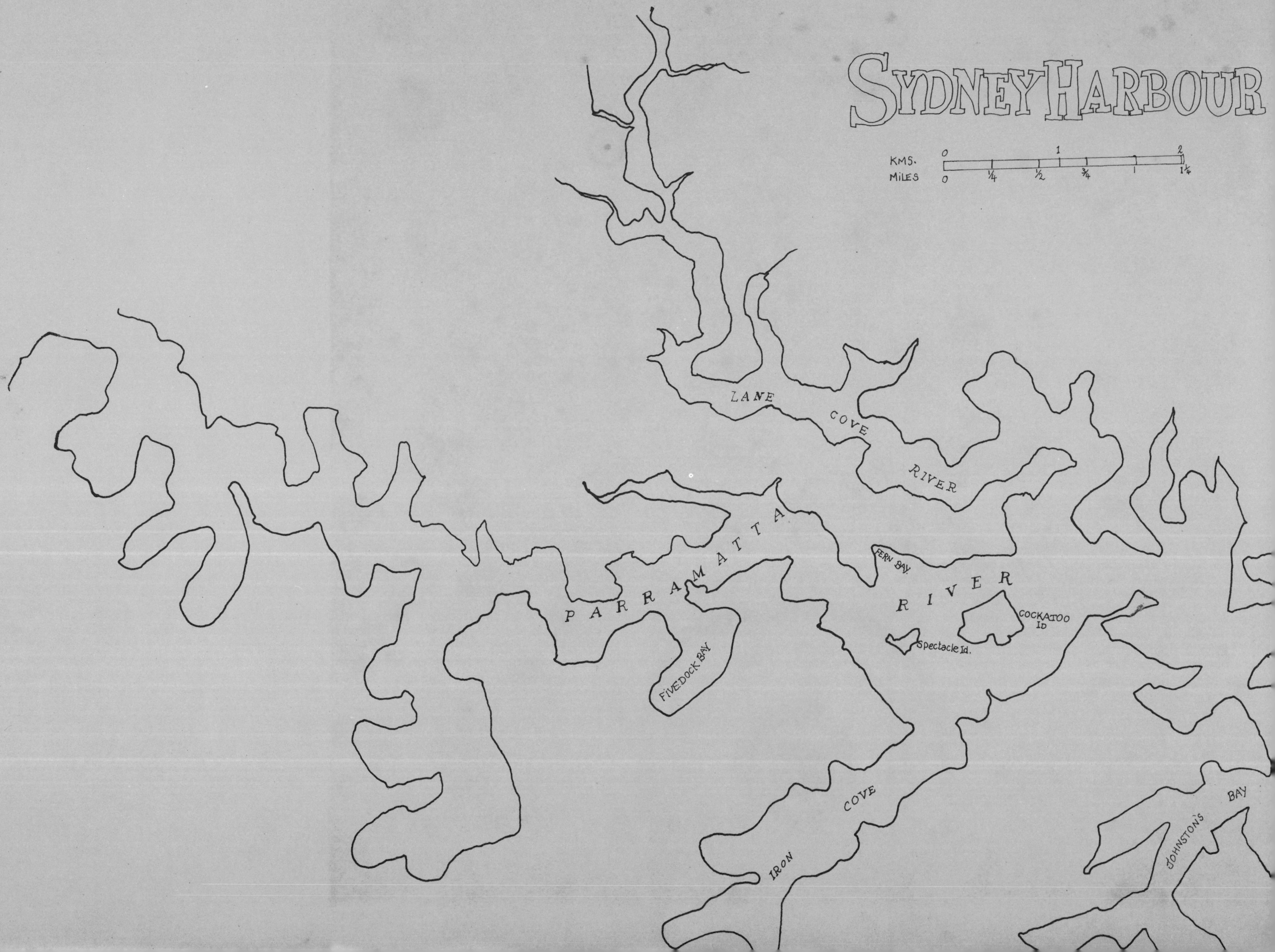
SYDNEY HARBOUR
KMS. 0 1 2
MILES 0 1/4 1/2 3/4 1 1 1/4
LANE COVE RIVER
PARRAMATTA RIVER
FERN BAY
COCKATOO ID
Spectacle Id.
FIVEDOCK BAY
IRON COVE
JOHNSTON'S BAY